Overcoming the 7 Battlefields of Marriage

A Biblical Practical Relationship Guide
for Singles & Married Couples

HURST HOUSE PUBLISHING

"Overcoming the 7 Battlefields of Marriage"

Overcoming the 7 Battlefields of Marriage

A Biblical Practical Relationship Guide
for Singles & Married Couples

GERMAINE D. HURST

Buffalo, New York

3

Library of Congress Control Number: 2020916863

ISBNs: 978-1-7356292-0-9 (paperback)
          978-1-7356292-1-6 (ebook)
          978-1-7356292-2-3 (study guide)

Printed in the United States of America

ABOUT THE AUTHOR

Germaine D. Hurst is a multi-dimensional leader who has devoted his life to changing lives. As an itinerant speaker and lecturer, he has travelled extensively throughout the country and abroad sharing his messages of hope and empowerment. He is an influential pastor, bishop, author and entrepreneur. His passion for ministry has afforded him the opportunity to build marriages, strengthen families and influence leaders for nearly three decades. As a yielded vessel he serves as the Senior Pastor and CEO of Greater Emmanuel Temple Church, Inc., "The Church of Champions" in Buffalo, NY, Founder of Germaine D. Hurst Ministries, Co-Founder of Heart 2 Hurst and Founder and CEO of Hurst House Publishing, LLC.

Follow Bishop Germaine D. Hurst
Facebook, Instagram, Twitter, Youtube: @pastorhurst
Email: speakhurst@gmail.com

DEDICATION

I would like to dedicate this book to my Queen, the one and only Denise C. Hurst. You have provided me with an excellent example to complete this book. I am thankful that you belong to me! I LOVE YOU!

To my incredible sons, "my four Gospels" that GOD has gifted to me, Jeremiah Christopher, Dynnell Alexander, Sean Joseph, and Zachery Jaden Hurst. I love you boys!

I dedicate this book to everyone that desires true love ordained by GOD. May this book be used as a tool to encourage you to build a successful relationship that will stand the test of time! May GOD bless you and yours!

ACKNOWLEDGEMENT

I would like to take this opportunity to acknowledge my "DADDY GOD". HE is the reason why I was given this assignment. I am nothing without YOU! YOU are everything to me. The Grace of my LORD and SAVIOR JESUS CHRIST has set the platform for my destiny. Thank you LORD for choosing me to do this! I love YOU!

Denise you are my secret weapon & Love of my Life. You are such an inspiration to me. Your love, support and encouragement refreshes my soul everyday. I love you Baby!

Thank you to all of my family, friends and the greatest church in the world, Greater Emmanuel Temple Church, Inc., "The Church of Champions". Thank you for helping me to grow as a Man of GOD and being a part of my Kingdom Process! I love you all!

PREFACE

This book is a response to the dilemma of marriages and relationships ending in such great devastation. For years, especially in the United States of America, there has been a relentless divorce rate. There is a pathology of infidelity and a lack of commitment when it comes to marriage vows and building lasting relationships.

Why is this happening? Maybe we lack the tools we need to succeed in relationships. Could it be the media and how it persuades our perception of what a good relationship should consist of? Is it possible that times have just changed and chivalry is dead? Is courtship a place where athletes gather and dating is dinner, dancing, movies and maybe some casual sex? These are all factors that contribute to the decline of lasting relationships. This book was written to deal with these challenges and provide answers to the issues that we face.

There are seven battlefields of marriage and this book presents biblical and practical principles of how to overcome them. The primary reason why

I wrote this book was to help eradicate many of the taboos, misconceptions, and misinformation associated with being married. I wanted to emphasize the need for strategy and perseverance in building a successful relationship.

I have been in ministry for thirty years. I am "happily" married to my high school sweetheart for twenty-two years. Prior to our marriage, we had a seven year courtship that I believe has prepared us for success in our relationship today. As a college graduate in Human Services & Psychology with a focus on Marriage & Family Living and Sociology, I realize the necessity of having coaches and mentors for marriage and relationship success.

The church is a microcosm of our society in which our faith doesn't exempt us from the challenges of relationships. The divorce rate in the church is just as high as the secular world. At the end of the day, "People will be people" whether you are a part of a religious institution or not. This book transcends religion and secular ideology.

My prayer is that as you read this book, GOD will illuminate your mind and provide insight on how to overcome the obstacles in marriage. May you be provoked into some actions that will better your relationships and propel you into a future filled with purpose and destiny. So READ, and be changed and challenged!

TABLE OF CONTENTS

ABOUT THE AUTHOR

DEDICATION

ACKNOWLEDGMENTS

PREFACE

CHAPTER 1

BATTLEFIELD #1 - COMMUNICATION

Communication is the first battlefield that we must overcome. It is the absolute foundation and hub of a relationship. Many couples fail in this area. No marriage can succeed without healthy effective communication. Attempting to build a relationship without healthy communication is virtually impossible. Many of us focus on sex, intimacy, money, and dating as the pinnacle of relationship success but communication trumps them all.

Our relationship with GOD is not physical but spiritual. It is 100% based on communication. We praise, pray and worship to communicate our love to HIM. Even though we have never physically seen or touched GOD, we believe that we are in a committed relationship with HIM based on our communication. In the Bible GOD is called the WORD in St. John 1:1. It is through the WORD that we have developed a healthy relationship with GOD. This same principle applies to us in our relationship with the ones we love. Communication is the foundation in which all relationships should build upon. We must maximize our communication skills in order to build a strong marriage. It is the playbook and strategy that will lead us to a winning relationship.

What does it mean to communicate?

Communication is simply sharing, understanding and connecting with others. The focus of our communication in marriage is to establish a foundation of sharing, understanding and connecting together as one. Healthy effective dialogue should be the primary focus for communicating with your spouse. Avoid negative and abusive words. As a child I remember saying, "Sticks and stones may break my bones but words will never hurt me." Boy, was I wrong! Many marriages are destroyed because of negative and abusive words. We should strive to communicate and connect with our spouses in a healthy manner.

Be careful about what you say.

Proverbs 18:21 - "Death and life are in the power of the tongue: and they that love it shall eat the fruit thereof."

There is power in our tongues and we must be careful of how we use it. I am encouraging you to speak life into your marriage and death to anything that will try to destroy it. My wife is such a blessing to me. We decided that the "D" word is not an option for us. We call divorce the "D" word. We refuse to even acknowledge it as a word or option in our marriage. Our words have power to kill and to make alive.

Your relationship will benefit by speaking life into each other. The bible says in *Hebrews 11:3, "Through faith we understand that the worlds were framed by the word of God, so that things which are seen were not made of things which do appear."* We frame our world through the words that we speak every day. What does your world look like? Does it look like what you say? Maybe our relationships are full of negative energy because of the words that we articulate. Sometimes it is not what we say but it is how we say it. What are we communicating to the mind, body and soul of the one that we love? Please understand that your words do make a difference. If you don't believe it, then read your bible and see how everything came into existence.

Our spouses need our continual support and affirmations. Speaking positive words into the life of your spouse will manifest results. Our words are like seeds that are sown in soil and whatever we sow will grow and be multiplied back to us. It is called the law of reciprocity.

We must be cautious about what we say. An argument or heated exchange of negative words can be very detrimental to a marriage. The bible warns us about our communication...

Psalms 141:3 - *"Set a watch, O LORD, before my mouth; keep the door of my lips."*

James 1:19 - *"Wherefore, my beloved brethren, let every man be swift to hear, slow to speak, slow to wrath:"*

Proverbs 15:1 - *"A soft answer turneth away wrath: but grievous words stir up anger."*

Negative and hurtful words can be forgiven but never taken back. They are like feathers blowing in the wind out of an open sack never to return. Use wisdom by exercising discretion in communication with the person that you love.

Understanding Our Communication differences

Husbands and wives can speak the same language but differ in understanding. We often speak and hear differently from each other. Here are some examples of our communication differences:

#1 What do we listen out for during communication?

Women: Men typically listen out for respect and honor. It is important that men do not feel disrespected or emasculated during a conversation. It is a turn off when men feel this way. Men love to be praised and honored. They will shut down or become confrontational when they feel disrespected. The testosterone will kick in and the conversation will be viewed as a challenge to their manhood. This is a terrible position to be in when trying to communicate with your husband.

Men: Women often listen out for love, appreciation, and acceptance. A lot of what is spoken to them must be connected to love and affection. Even if there is a disagreement, it must be done in the spirit of love. Women have a keen

23

sense of emotion and feelings through words and conversations. She formulates opinions based on your communication with her. Love is an essential element in the conversation that she needs to hear and feel from you. It is not always about what we say but it is how we say it! If all she hears and feels is disappointment, disapproval and rejection then the outcome will be very detrimental to the relationship.

Whatever you give a women will be multiplied and given back to you. A wise man once told me, "Give a woman groceries and she will give you a meal, give her your seed and she will give you a child, give her grief and she will give you damnation!" This is funny, but true. Remember to give each other respect and love during communication.

#2 **What is the goal of the conversation?**

Women: The goal of most men in a conversation is to come to a direct solution to fix the problem or dilemma. He wants to get straight to the point and find a solution. Your husband would rather talk about how to fix what is wrong instead of trying to find out why it is wrong. The husband sees his wife as a pilot flying a plane in the conversation.

All he wants is for her to land it! Even if she crashes, he will rescue her from the flames and wreckage. He will try to be the hero and fix what "he" feels is the problem. Men feel valued when they fix things. This approach is often short cited because even though he found a solution, it doesn't mean that he fixed the problem. Encourage him to take the time through communication to find out your "why". This will demonstrate that he cares about how you are feeling.

Men: Her goal is getting understanding. She doesn't want to get solutions without understanding. She wants you to connect with her feelings. It is important to her that you understand what is going on in her mind and heart without trying to fix things. Be open to communicate and connect with her feelings. The problem does exist but try to be there for her. Acknowledge her feelings and empathize.

#3 What we do when the conversation is frustrating us?

Women: Men generally become silent and not very talkative. This is very frustrating because you really want him to talk even if it provokes an argument or a reaction. Many women may feel that men are not emotional but that is not true. Men are emotional but they emote differently from women. Some men have the gift of gab and can go back and forth with a woman and the argument just gets worse. Some men just become completely silent. At this point he is having an internal conversation within himself and not with her. He is deliberately not speaking to his spouse because:

1) To inflict non-verbal pain by ignoring and neglecting her need to communicate her feelings.

2) To avoid further verbal confrontation.

3) He does not know what to say or how to say it without a fight.

4) He is having a non-verbal stand-off to show that he is upset and disapproves of her in order to get the upper hand to control the situation.

The silent treatment is very dangerous over a long period of time. Taking a break or breather from communication to be civil and calm is good but using it as a weapon is not wise.

Men: Women generally will give the silent treatment but they really want to talk. They become very upset when the dialogue doesn't happen. They are often ready and willing to verbalize their frustration. The English playwright William Congreve wrote in "The Mourning Bride (1697)", "Heaven has no rage, like love to hatred turned, Nor hell a fury, like a woman scorned." Anger is a pure emotion that one may feel, but it is how we deal with those feelings and how we react that determines our maturity. A wise solution is to defuse anger as soon as possible and have a calm conversation that is not driven by anger. The bible declares in *Ephesians 4:26*, *"Be ye angry, and sin not: let not the sun go down upon your wrath."* Do your best to deescalate the situation instead of going to bed angry. Continuous silent treatment and temper tantrums with no resolve is unproductive and a waste of time. Remember to manage your emotions because you are in control of them!

#4 What is our motivation for conversation?

Women: A situation is needed to motivate men to have a conversation. Men are primarily reactive when engaging in communication with their spouse. Being proactive will satisfy the need to engage in conversation. The right situation will cause him to open up and express his feelings on a subject matter or situation. Be open to discuss what interests him. Allow the conversation to be organic and unrehearsed.

Men: Women are extremely motivated by conversation and connecting. They are more calculated through communication which motivates them to engage in conversation. They like to connect all of the dots and have a discussion. A wife will ask her husband many questions to calculate her perceived outcome of a situation. She connects past behavior with a current situation to determine how she should feel. Keep her love tank full by engaging in daily conversation.

Five Keys to Healthy Effective Communication

I.C.A.R.E.

I would like to take this opportunity to give you five keys to healthy effective communication in a relationship. These keys should be used as tools to overcome the battlefield of communication. These keys are exemplified through the acronym "I.C.A.R.E."

Key #1: "I" - Be Intentional: It is important that communication with your mate is intentional and purposeful. Every discussion should have a desired outcome even if it is an argument or disagreement.

Be willing to pick your battles because you can win an argument but lose a mate. Be intentional and count the spoils to see if its worth the debate. Using time and words with no desired outcome in the end is a complete waste of time. Our content must have intent. What ever you say, do it on "PURPOSE".

Key #2: "C" - Be Courteous: Be courteous to your mate. Being respectful and considerate goes a long way in communication. Never say anything in your anger that you will regret later. Remember that you are speaking to someone that you love. Be polite to your spouse. Being courteous during a disagreement is like placing water on a flame of fire instead of gasoline.

Key #3: "A" - Be Attentive: Be willing to do more listening than speaking. Stop waiting for your spouse to stop talking so you can have your turn to speak without any regard for what they just shared. Try your best to understand and receive from them. Use eye contact and affirmations. Being attentive shows that you care about what your spouse is saying.

Key #4: "R" - Be Respectful: The Queen of Soul, the Late Aretha Franklin sung the hit song, "R-E-S-P-E-C-T"! Don't give them, "Just a little bit," but always respect your spouse to the fullest. Respect and honor will get you access. It is a powerful tool to use in communication. We respect those who we honor and cherish. Your spouse is valuable and should be respected. They should be number one and be treated as such. Our spouses should be our priority.

Key #5: "E" - Be Expressive: Your thoughts and feelings matter and need to be expressed. How you express yourself to your spouse is personal. Expression is an art that needs to be mastered in order to have true freedom in your relationship. The opportunity to express yourself should never be taken away from you or your mate. It is abusive to deny your spouse the opportunity to express themselves. The lack of expression is a denial of effective communication. Remember to always express yourself!

What does he need her to say?

Women: Every man needs to hear his companion express how important and valuable he is to her. Tell him that he is a great provider and that you trust him. Speak what you believe him to be and want him to become in the marriage. Let him know that he is your King and that you feel safe and secure with him. Compliment him on his hard work and motivate him to continue. Speak and encourage him daily. Most men will hasten to perform in order to receive praise from someone that they love and respect. Ladies, always speak to "your man" with respect even if you have a disagreement and never compare him to other men. Learn to verbalize your frustration without being accused of "nagging". If you make him feel like he is the man, he will act like it!

What does she need him to say?

Men: Women want their spouse to express their feelings, love and appreciation for them. Tell her that you love and admire her. She wants you to express your thoughts and engage in conversation as much as possible. Your wife feels important and special when you share with her. Tell her that she is beautiful and sexy and that you want her.

Making phone calls and texting is important to her. Let her know that you are thinking about her and can't wait to see her. Acknowledge that you are interested in what she is doing and what she has to say. Men, if she needs to unload her day to you, LET HER! Smile and give positive feed back and show concern and confirm that you understand. Even though you may have a shorter attention span, she wants it all. Do not compare her to any other women. Always encourage and compliment her. Make sure you notice the small things and pay attention to detail. Your encouragement means a lot to her. Constantly remind her that she is your Queen that you love her.

Conclusion

The Battlefield of Communication is the greatest challenge of all 7 battlefields. Master the art of communication with your spouse in order to have a happy marriage. Healthy effective communication in your relationships will certainly build a very strong union. Remember to speak life into each other!

NOTES

CHAPTER 2

BATTLEFIELD #2 - SEX

Genesis 2:25 "And they were both naked, the man and his wife, and were not ashamed."

The topic of sex is considered to be taboo in many circles. I often say that there are two things that people feel uncomfortable with talking about, but want to have it all of the time... MONEY & SEX! Sex is very important in a marriage. Every couple should strive for a healthy sex life. It is an intimate way of sharing and communicating with your spouse. There are many couples that struggle in this area. Sex is a battlefield that must be addressed in order for a couple to have true fulfillment and satisfaction.

Sex is not dirty!

It is imperative that we understand that sex is not dirty. Sex is GOD's gift to us to express our love to our spouses. HE ordained it for marriage and it is sacred. Sex is beautiful and is meant to be shared between two individuals that are joined together in holy matrimony.

Always remember that what you share in the bedroom with your spouse is private. Your spouse is the only one that should know you sexually which is the highest level of intimacy. Sex is not sinful, unclean or dirty. It is when two people become one in the eyes of GOD. Many christians are worried about becoming defiled through sexual intercourse but the Bible says in **Hebrews 13:4,** *"Marriage is honourable in all, and the bed undefiled: but whoremongers and adulterers God will judge."* Defiled means spoiled. Once a couple is lawfully married, sex is considered pure in GOD's eyes and that marriage is honorable. It is important that your sexual relationship with your spouse remain personal. Don't allow people into your bedroom by sharing your personal sex life with them. Guard your intimacy and the connection that you share with the one you love.

REMEMBER TO K.I.S.S.

Remember to "**K.I.S.S.**" your spouse in order to have a healthy sex life. **K.I.S.S.** is the acronym for **Knowledge, Intimacy, Sensuality, & Sacrifice.**

#1 - KNOWLEDGE

1 Peter 3:7 *"Likewise, ye husbands, dwell with them according to knowledge, giving honour unto the wife, as unto the weaker vessel, and as being heirs together of the grace of life; that your prayers be not hindered."*

It is important that we have knowledge about our mates. We should know what turns them off and on. Getting to know each other is paramount when it comes to sexual fulfillment. Knowing how to communicate and paying attention to detail will take you a long way. What are your spouse's interests? What are they attracted to? What do they like and dislike? What makes them happy? These are all important questions that need to be answered. Familiarize yourself with your spouse's body, soul and spirit. Make it your priority to dwell with them according to knowledge.

Getting to know your mate's likes and dislikes in the bedroom is important. Never force them to do anything that they don't want to do! Sex with your spouse should be enjoyable for the both of you. Make sure that he or she feels loved and not abused or objectified.

What does he need to know?

Men: Women are like crockpots and men are like microwaves. Men are ready for a sexual encounter within a split second and women are the polar opposite. She needs him to take his time and "SLOW DOWN". She needs communication, intimacy, attention and affection. Sex begins in the heart and mind of a woman and not in the bedroom. Let her know how much you love her and how special she is to you. Intimacy is the key.

What does she need to know?

Women: Sex is extremely important for a man. Sex to a man is like carbon dioxide to a plant. It is something that he needs and not just wants. Do not deprive him of sex. When you are married your body is no longer your own. It belongs to your husband and he belongs to you. Communicate with your husband. Inform him that you need him to get you into the mood. This is done by coaching and expressing to him your need for intimacy and affection. Continuously rejecting sex is unhealthy for the marriage. You never want your husband looking over the fence for spoils. Let him know that everything he needs is with you! Be spontaneous and communicate that you desire him.

#2 - INTIMACY

Song of Solomon 1:2 *"Let him kiss me with the kisses of his mouth:for thy love is better than wine."*

Sex and intimacy are two different things. Intimacy is not a prerequisite for sex. Intimacy is the art of making love without sexual intercourse. It is the opportunity to express your love for your spouse by being affectionate. Holding hands, texting each other, love notes, kissing, hugging, cuddling and making phone calls and saying, "I love you" are all ways to fill the love tank of intimacy.

#3 - SENSUALITY

1 Corinthians 7:33 *"But he that is married careth for the things that are of the world, how he may please his wife."*

Sensuality is very important when it comes to

sexually pleasing your spouse. It deals specifically with your five senses which is sight, sound, taste, touch and smell. These are the five pleasure centers that stimulate attraction, arousal and erotic desire. Every spouse wants to feel and be wanted by their mate.

What does she need to know?

Women: Men are very visual and are stimulated primarily through sight and touch. Ladies, give your husband something to look at to be desired. It is important that you keep yourself looking good both in and out of the bedroom. Dress appealing and keep yourself up. Wearing curlers, head scarfs, bonnets, skin cream etc. has its place but be mindful that it is not attractive to your husband. Make sure you balance that out. Wearing lingerie and sexual revealing garments for him is a plus. Your hair, feet and nails should be clean and well manicured. Perfume, scented lotions, and body wash will only encourage him to draw closer to you. Never be afraid to be sensual. You have a natural beauty that he desires. GOD made you that way!

What does he need to know?

Men: A women loves to see and touch but they are primarily stimulated by sound and smell. Any man that stinks and fails to have good conversation is a turn off. Taking showers, having fresh breath, wearing cologne, deodorant, and being well dressed is attractive to her. Being romantic and communicating makes her feel special. Remind her that she is beautiful and that you belong together. Presenting her with gifts, flowers, candy and cards/ notes will set the mood and the tone for romance.

Our sensual side calls for us to be healthy and take care of our bodies. Sexual attraction is different for everyone. We all have different body shapes, sizes and personalities. Find out what your spouse likes and pursue it. Being sensual is not a sin. GOD made you that way. Only reserve it for your spouse and not for everyone else.

#4 - SACRIFICE

Ephesians 5:28-29 *"So ought men to love their wives as their own bodies. He that loveth his wife loveth himself. For no man ever yet hated his own flesh; but nourisheth and cherisheth it, even as the Lord the church."*

Sexual intercourse with your spouse is sacred.

41

This act is only meant for the married. Sexual fulfillment is obtained by both parties not being selfish. You must be willing to sacrifice your own fleshly desires to please your spouse.

What does he need to know?

Men: Ladies first! Men it is important to understand that most women are capable of having multiple orgasms. Sacrifice your own instant gratification and take the time to please your wife first. Foreplay helps to slow the sexual experience. Kissing and caressing stimulates her body. Be sure to communicate with her about what she wants during the experience. Cater to her needs while fulfilling yours. Remember that both of you should have pleasure.

What does she need to know?

Women: How you look and present yourself is important. Respecting your husband and honoring him is pivotal. Kissing and coming close to him to caress is desirable to him. He is always ready for you! He needs you to help him pace the experience. Slow him down! It is important to compliment him by letting him know that he is pleasing you during intimacy.

Five Types of Intimacy

#1 Emotional Intimacy is the sharing of your feelings and emotions with your spouse. You share the good, the bad and the ugly. Crying on their shoulder or sharing your happiness and/or anger is safe with them. You are not afraid of being vulnerable with your partner because they protect your feelings. Sharing how we feel with our spouses is very intimate and needs to be protected.

#2 Intellectual Intimacy is the ability to discuss and exchange ideas and things you care deeply about without judgement. Who can I share my heart and head with? Engaging in meaningful conversation on an intellectual level can be very intimate. Guard your personal thoughts and conversations with each other. Remember that you should not share your business with everyone. There are some things that should only be reserved for your spouse. Never breach your confidentiality as a couple.

#3 Physical Intimacy is being physically affectionate with your spouse without having sex. It is a level of physical encounter that is only reserved for them. Some examples are kissing, holding hands, massages, hugging, cuddling, and intimate touches.

#4 Experiential Intimacy is having an experience with the one you love that is only meant for them. You make them feel special through an experience or event free from interruption of others. An example could be a get-away like a cruise, going to dinner at their favorite restaurant, going on a date, holding hands and taking a long walk or a drive. It is all about the experience that generates a memory and a feeling of love towards your spouse. The focus is not the bedroom but it is all about the experience that you share.

#5 Spiritual Intimacy is developing an inner connection with your spouse that is built on your faith and relationship with GOD. You both pray with each other and seek GOD for guidance in your marriage. You fall in love with each other on a spiritual level. Worshipping and praying together in your home will establish an intimate spiritual connection with each other.

50 THINGS THAT HINDER
SEXUAL FULFILLMENT IN A MARRIAGE

#1   The Presence of Children - Be sure that children are not in close proximity during sexual encounters. Many spouses, primarily women have a tough time getting in the mood when children are around. Children will interrupt the moment. Put them to bed, move them, move yourself or reschedule to avoid this issue.

#2   Sickness & Disease - Treat and medicate all illnesses that will hinder your sexual performance.

#3   Depression & Anxiety - Mental illness and chemical imbalances will effect the mood. Sex is physical as well as mental. Seek proper treatment and counsel if needed.

#4   Impotency - The inability to have and maintain an erection can hinder sex. Medication or medical attention may be needed to resolve this issue.

#5   Arguments - Unresolved conflicts need to be dealt with and resolved.

#6   Cheating & Infidelity - Be loyal to your spouse and save yourself only for them.

#7   **Disrespect** - Be considerate and respect each other.

#8   **Dirty** - Be sure to be clean and sanitary.

#9   **Fatigue** - Get plenty of rest and adequate sleep.

#10   **No Intimacy** - Make time for each other. Be romantic and engage in at least one of the five types of intimacy.

#11   **Lack of Communication** - Speak to each other and engage in healthy conversation.

#12   **Bad Timing & Location** - Work with each others schedule and make time for each other. Find a safe and secure place that makes you comfortable.

#13   **Emasculating** - Don't dominate over your spouse and deprive them of masculinity.

#14   **Lack of Focus** - Focus on the moment with your spouse and nothing else.

#15   **Boredom & Lack of Versatility** - Don't be afraid to do something different. Add some excitement to the relationship by bringing energy to the bedroom. Don't be afraid to be spontaneous.

#16   **Unforgiveness** - Stop holding grudges and being bitter toward each other.

#17   Lack of Privacy - Mind your own business and keep people out of yours. Remember that what happens in your bedroom should stay in your bedroom.

#18   Lack of Foreplay - Give your spouse something to look forward to. Flirt, touch, kiss and explore each other.

#19   Premature Ejaculation - Don't be overly excited. Slow down and take your time!

#20   Inappropriate Engagement - Don't force your spouse to do anything that they disagree with or feel uncomfortable doing.

#21   Evil Imagination - Fantasizing about someone else while having sex with your spouse is inappropriate.

#22   Business Transaction - Giving your spouse sex in exchange for goods and services is inappropriate.

#23   Control - Using sex or the lack thereof to control your spouse to get what you want is inappropriate.

#24   Pain & Discomfort - Making love should be pleasurable for both parties and not traumatizing.

#25   Sexual Abuse - A traumatic past history of rape, molestation and sexual abuse can effect sexual intercourse with your spouse. This needs to be addressed with patience, compassion, counsel, and prayer for inner healing. In some cases law enforcement may be necessary.

#26   Fear & Shame - Overcome being afraid, timid and shameful with your spouse. Adam and Eve were both naked and not ashamed. - **Genesis 2:25**

#27   Inexperience - Virginity or lack of experience may be an issue with your spouse. Understand the more you engage in sex with your spouse the more you will learn. Take your time and don't rush anything. Communicating and being comfortable with each other is key.

#28   Promiscuity - Having a history of frequent sex with different sex partners can hinder your current relationship. Don't bring your past into your future. Don't allow previous relationships to hinder your current one.

#29   Physical Fitness - Obesity and/or too much weight loss can effect your performance because sex takes energy. Stay balanced and healthy.

#30   Drug & Alcohol Abuse - Chemical dependency effects sexual performance and can cause other issues that hinder sexual fulfillment.

#31   Piousness - Being overly spiritual with carnal things is not good. Never be so heavenly bound that you are no earthly good! Remember that sex is earthly and carnal. There will be no sex in heaven.

#32   Perversion - Abnormal sexual behavior and experimenting with ungodly lust is inappropriate.

#33   Pornography - Indulging in explicit entertainment that encourages masturbation, lust and evil imagination towards someone that doesn't belong to you is inappropriate.

#34   Being a Eunuch - A Eunuch is someone who doesn't have sexual desire and will not engage. It is possible to marry someone who does not want to have sex. You should know this before you marry them.

#35   Undisclosed Homosexuality (Down Low) - Some spouses could be secretly attracted to the same sex and refuse to engage in heterosexual behavior. Get to know your partner before you marry them.

#36 Menstrual Cycle - Women's bodies go through a hormonal process every month that hinders sexual intercourse.

#37 No Orgasm - Failure to have a sexual climax during intercourse may discourage engagement. Communicate with your partner about finding G-spots and doing what is needed to encourage climax.

#38 No Attraction - Feeling that your spouse is unattractive can hinder the desire to have sex. Communication and discovering what attracts your spouse is helpful.

#39 Birth Control - Be sure that you discuss with your mate on whether or not they want to have children. Sex may be avoided due to the lack of birth control or the fear of getting pregnant. Some people may be putting themselves in a medical risk if they get pregnant. Make sure you communicate with each other and consult a physician.

#40 Fear of Rejection - Don't confuse "not now" with "never". There may be times when there are legitimate reasons to not have sex. However, try to say yes more than no. Remember that continually turning your spouse away may lead to them no longer asking or wanting to engage in sex to avoid rejection.

#41   Age - Age does effect ones sex life both mentally and physically. Sexual compatibility with your spouse can depend on age. One may be significantly older or younger than the other. Your body will respond differently.

#42   Performance - It is possible to have an unfulfilling sexual experience with your spouse. Communication is very important. Discuss ways to improve your sex life with your spouse.

#43   Prolonged Climax - Don't be too long getting to climax. Never unnecessarily prolong sex for the sake of time parameters. Be mindful that prolonging can be viewed just as bad as being premature.

#44   Lack of Passion - Your spouse doesn't want to make love to a "Zombie" or a "Mannequin". Show emotion and express that you are enjoying the moment.

#45   Laziness - Having sex with your spouse shouldn't feel like a chore or a one person job. Laziness is a mood killer. It sends a message to your spouse that they would rather do something else.

#46   Negative Criticism - Don't be negative or condescending to your spouse. Try to stay positive.

#47   Making Comparisons - Never compare your spouse with previous lovers! Making comparisons brings other people into your bedroom.

#48   Life's Problems - Life is full of problems, trouble and disappointments. Do your best to not bring them into your intimate space.

#49   Busyness - Make time for each other. Remember that you are never too busy to make love.

#50   Financial Strain - There is a saying, "There can be no romance without finance." Financial challenges can put a strain on a relationship. Build a strong relationship in the absence of money. Remind yourself that you do it better together. Money comes and goes but your love for each other should remain.

Conclusion

Sex should be centered around intimacy and love. Keep your sex life sacred by protecting it from others. It is your place of peace, serenity and pleasure. Remember that sex is not dirty. Avoid infidelity and the trappings of temptation. Your sexual intimacy should remain exclusive and fulfilling.

<u>NOTES</u>

_____

_____

_____

_____

_____

_____

_____

_____

_____

_____

_____

_____

_____

_____

CHAPTER 3

BATTLEFIELD #3 - MONEY

Ecclesiastes 7:11-12 *"For wisdom is a defence, and money is a defence: but the excellency of knowledge is, that wisdom giveth life to them that have it."*

Marriage and money our two things that are difficult to manage. Anything that we fail to manage we will lose. Money is a defense and can protect us from many issues. However, having money without wisdom can be very detrimental. The most common area of disagreement and conflict in marriages is money. Financial issues in marriage are the leading cause of divorce. It is important that we manage our money in order to avoid unnecessary stress and pressure. Wisdom is the key to financial success within a marriage.

Understanding the 3 Types of Money Handlers

There are three types of money handlers. Money is a servant that should obey it's handlers. We must pay close attention to how we handle our money. Each money handler has pros and cons.

The focus should be balance and not extremes. Identifying what type of money handler you are is half the battle. Don't be afraid to acknowledge your money habits. Communicating with your spouse in this area will better help you to formulate a strategy on how to handle finances.

Money Handler #1: The Spenders

You are most likely a spender if you do the following:

- Shop to fill an emotional void to be happy.

- You are an impulsive buyer.

- Feeling that you must have the latest fashions, gadgets and products even though it causes you to be broke.

- Constantly swiping your debit and/or credit cards without knowing your balances.

- Purchasing items that you can't afford.

- Fails to reconcile or balance your checkbook or account.

- Often has insufficient funds and bounces checks.

- Feels depressed if you can't purchase what you want at the moment.

- Enjoys eating out and attending events that uses money.

- Maxing out all credit cards and still desires more.

- Believes that money is meant to be spent to get what you want.

- Loves going on trips, vacations, and spas that you can't afford.

- More outgoing, unconstrained and enjoys life without counting up the cost.

- Rarely has money on hand for emergencies.

Money Handler #2: The Savers

You are most likely a saver if you do the following:

- Is anxious and uncomfortable when spending money.

- Wears old worn clothing and shoes until they fall apart.

- Uses old gadgets and technology until it breaks.

- Procrastinates when making purchases or spending money.

- Often has buyers remorse and would rather hold the money than spend it.

- Always shops the clearance section and uses coupons and discounts.

- Never swipes the debit and/or credit card without knowing the balance.

- Gets happy when money is deposited in the savings account and has anxiety when it leaves.

- Would rather be a homebody instead of going out and spending money.

- Is considered cheap by others.

- Normally waits and budgets for major purchases.

- More reserved, sensible, cautious and conservative when it comes to finances.

Money Handlers #3: The Givers

You are most likely a giver if you do the following:

- You are very generous toward others.

- Gets joy out of sharing with others.

- Gives even if it hurts.

- Very compassionate to those in need.

- Feels uncomfortable not helping others.

- Gets frustrated when you can't give to others.

- Others are depending on your generosity.

- Doesn't want to see anyone struggle.

- Finds ways to give when you can't afford it.

- Doesn't do well receiving from others.

- Would rather give than receive.

- Thinks of others during holidays, special occasions, birthdays etc.

- Doesn't spend much money on yourself.

- Doesn't maintain adequate savings due to giving to others.

- Rarely gets paid back when others borrow.

All three of these ways of handling money have pros and cons. In most relationships, there is a spender and saver. It is true that opposites do attract. It is your assignment to understand and overcome your differences. Every marriage consists of at least one of these handling styles. The most important thing is to manage and work together in order to thrive financially. Remember that balance is the key.

Marriage is a Union and Partnership!

Every marriage should be viewed as a union and partnership. You do it better together! Here are a few suggestions and keys to assist you in the area of money management in your relationship.

15 Money Management Keys in a Relationship

Key #1 Communication: Talking about money is important. Often times, the lack of money is the result of the lack of communication. It is normal to have disagreements about finances. Make sure that you listen to each other and try to come up with solutions by talking about money.

Key #2 Honesty: Being transparent and honest about your finances is important. Every couple should be aware of each others debts and finances. Do you know each others FICO Score? How much debt do each of you owe? What is on your credit reports? How much money do you both have saved? Do you have any secret accounts or purchases? Are you hiding anything from your spouse? All of these are questions that should be answered honestly.

Key #3 Accountability: Taking responsibility for the finances of your home is paramount. Stop casting the blame on each other. Be accountable to each other and set your standards and expectations. All financial accounts should have accountability.

Key #4 Know Your Credit Score: TransUnion, Experian and Equifax are the three major Credit Reporting Agencies within the United States. They record data pertaining to your employment status, creditors, debts and payment history. Your debt ratio, repayment history, and credit utilization determines what is called your FICO Score. This score determines approvals for bank loans, credit cards, employment, leasing, and renting property to name a few. The Credit Agencies record your data and puts it on your credit report and then generates your FICO Score which determines your range of credit and/or borrowing risk. **(See List)**

The FICO Score Range List:

Exceptional	(800-850)
Very Good	(740-799)
Good	(670-739)
Fair	(580-669)
Very Poor	(300-579)

There are free apps that you can download like Credit Karma and Credit Sesame that will provide your FICO Score. Take the time to know your score before attempting to apply for credit or loans.

Key #5 Set Financial Goals: Failure in setting financial goals is like shooting a dart with no bullseye! Communicate your financial future with each other. Make goals and milestones for your financial journey. You must know where you are going and how to get there.

Key #6 Establish a Budget: Having a budget directs your money where to go. We lose whatever we fail to manage. Manage your streams by determining what is coming in and what is going out. Budgeting is the key to financial success.

Key #7 "Marry" Some of Your Bank Accounts: I encourage married couples to combine some of their money and establish an expense account to push you towards financial freedom. This account is used strictly to handle all expenses and debts together with your combined revenue. More can be accomplished this way by working together instead of separating your finances. However, in addition to the expense account, it is okay for you and your partner to have personal accounts that you both have agreed upon to use at your own discretion. This will help to avoid conflicts and control issues with money.

Key #8 Create a Small Emergency Fund: Having an emergency fund is very wise. You never know when a "rainy day" will come. We are human and live in a world where emergencies will arise. BE PREPARED! An emergency fund of at least $1,000 should be saved. This fund should be used for emergencies only. When using the emergency fund please remember to replenish what was used as soon as possible.

Key #9 Eliminate Debt: The Financial Advisor Dave Ramsey speaks about using the "Debt Snowball" method to eliminate debt. This concept is very effective. This method begins with paying off the smallest bill to the largest. After paying off each debt, apply the same payment towards the next debt until paid off. Eliminating debt as soon as possible is imperative. Use any method that may work for you to eliminate debt.

Key #10 Establish Short & Long Term Savings:

It is important that you pay yourself and your bills. Establish a short and long term savings plan. **Short Term Savings** is money that is saved for short term goals and shorter periods of time like 3 to 6 months. This type of savings is good for vacations, holidays and preparing for special purchases etc. **Long Term Savings** is money that is placed in reserves for the long haul for your future like retirement or buying a home. It is important that you see the big picture and start saving now.

Key #11 Invest in Retirement: Remember to invest in your retirement. If you don't want to work all of your life then prepare to retire. There are 401k's, Roths, Roth IRA's and various retirement accounts to consider. Contact a financial advisor and find out what works for you and save.

Key #12 Develop Several Streams of Income:

Don't be satisfied with one stream of revenue. If one source dries up than make sure there are other streams. Remember that, "every rabbit has more than one hole to hide in." Be creative and consistent. Don't be afraid to start a business, invest, sell or pickup an additional job or a side hustle.

Key #13 Give to be a Blessing: Use your money to make a difference in the lives of others. The Law of Reciprocity works! Manage your finances in order to stay blessed. Remember that what you do for others does matter!

Key #14 Seek Investment Opportunities: Do your research and invest. Investing in real estate, stocks, and business ventures are a few ways to receive additional income. All investing has some form of risk. The saying, "Without risk there can be no reward.", is true!" Do not be afraid of taking a risk as long as that risk is calculated. Be wise and never invest out of the money that feeds you. Make sure to put some money to the side for investing and watch it grow over time.

Key #15 Manage Your Money with Percentages:

- **10%** of your money is your tithe that belongs to GOD. *Remember your local church or charitable giving toward others in need.*

- **10%** goes towards your savings. *Remember to pay yourself.*

- **5%** of your money should be for your personal development and education. *Remember to invest in yourself.*

- **5%** of your income should be saved for your children's education and future. *Remember to leave a legacy.*

- **10%** of your income is for your personal use and investing opportunities. *Remember to seek opportunities and let your money work for you.*

- **60%** of your income should go towards living expenses. *Remember that home comes first.*

Conclusion

Money should not be the source of your happiness within a marriage. Remember that it is a valuable resource to serve a need but not the source that fulfills all of your needs. Only GOD can fulfill all of your needs! **Philippians 4:19 NIV** *"And my God will meet all your needs according to the riches of his glory in Christ Jesus."*

Money is a means to an end and not the end all of all things. It will come and go but your love for each other should always remain. Your money is your servant and it should never become your master! All money should be managed, directed and invested in order to build wealth. May you build wealth upon the foundation of your love.

NOTES

_____

_____

_____

_____

_____

_____

_____

_____

_____

_____

_____

_____

_____

_____

_____

CHAPTER 4

BATTLEFIELD #4 - IN-LAWS

Genesis 2:24 *"Therefore shall a man leave his father and his mother, and shall cleave unto his wife: and they shall be one flesh."*

In-Laws or Outlaws

It is important to understand that there are no perfect families. Every family has their own culture, flaws and dysfunction. The goal of every married couple should be to build a positive relationship with your in-laws. This can be very challenging to accomplish when couples don't understand each others family dynamic.

All families are not easy to get a long with. Sometimes in-laws can be more like outlaws. They can be critical and unsupportive of your marriage. It may take time to develop a strong bond with your in-laws. Remember to never let family come between you and your spouse. Take the time to explore each others family culture and dynamic. Be open and honest with each other about how you feel about your families. Try to establish a bond with your in-laws by attending special family events like reunions, weddings, and funerals to demonstrate that you care and are a part of the family. Remember to use discretion when dealing with each others family. Wisdom is the key when developing healthy relationships with your in-laws.

Twelve Rules of Engaging Your In-Laws

Rule #1) Learn Each Other's Family Culture.

It is imperative to understand each other's family culture. The more you understand the better equipped you will be to deal with your in-laws. Never assume that you know your in-laws family culture. Properly engage them in conversation and social circles. Avoid stereotyping your in-laws. Everyone's family dynamic is different. Make sure you learn, observe, listen and make the proper adjustments. This is why courtship is so very important when developing relationships. Getting to know your in-laws is just as important as getting to know your spouse. Remember that you married into a family.

Rule #2) Don't Try to Change Your In-Laws.

It is not your responsibility to change your relatives! Avoid having a cavalier attitude when it comes to changing each other's family dynamic. This kind of behavior can lead to a conflict. Just like we cannot change the spots of a leopard or the stripes of a tiger neither do we have the power to change our in-laws.

Rule #3) Avoid Making Family Comparisons.

Try to complete and not compete with each other. Comparing families is not wise. All families are different and have strengths and weaknesses. Don't bombard and argue with each other by comparing family members. Nothing good will come out of that!

Rule #4) Set and Maintain Healthy Boundaries.

Don't allow your relatives to interfere with the standards and boundaries that you have set for your home. Family members have no right to dictate to you how you should operate or run your house. Establish your family culture and set a standard. If your family members will not respect your boundaries then they will not respect you.

Rule #5) Exercise Confidentiality.

Your personal business should remain private. Be very discreet about what you share with your family members. Whatever you decide to share make sure that your spouse is comfortable with that decision. Be sensitive to each others feelings and privacy.

Rule #6) Don't Spread Gossip and Rumors.

Stay clear of family drama. Don't be accused of being a busybody! This can lead to having a bad reputation with family members. Don't be the nosy, instigating family member that is always meddling in other peoples affairs. Be discreet, conservative and be a peacemaker in the family.

Rule #7) Prioritize Your Spouse.

Never prioritize your in-laws or family members before your spouse. Your spouse should be number one! No in-law or relative should come between the two of you. Inform your family that you love them but your spouse comes first.

Rule #8) Keep Family Out of Your Disputes.

It is unwise to allow family members to engage in disputes and arguments between you and your spouse. You may forgive your spouse but your family may hold a grudge. This will put a strain on your marriage. There will be times when you will disagree with each other. Don't sound the alarm in every disagreement or argument. However, violence and abuse is not tolerated and should not be ignored. Seek help immediately if you are being abused.

Rule #9) Don't Disrespect Your In-Laws.

Respect goes a long way. Disrespecting your in-laws is not wise. This kind of behavior leads to arguments and division. Respect your spouse by not disrespecting their family. If you have any concerns or issues with your in-laws, try to resolve them in a positive manner. Engage in healthy conflict resolution.

Rule #10) Keep a Positive Attitude.

There are no perfect families. You will not always see eye to eye. Remember that you have the power to manage your emotions. Don't allow minor setbacks to become major problems. Focus on the positive things and keep it moving. Trouble doesn't last always. Better days are coming!

Rule #11)   Protect and Defend Your Spouse.

It is imperative that you defend and protect your spouse at all times. Never allow your in-laws to pick on or bully your spouse. Guard your spouse from abusive situations. No one has the right to abuse the one you love. It is your responsibility to keep your family in check if they cross the line. Love and cherish your spouse at all times.

Rule #12)   Leave and Cleave!

Genesis 2:24 *"Therefore shall a man leave his father and his mother, and shall cleave unto his wife: and they shall be one flesh."*

Marriage gives you the right to leave and cleave. The word, "cleave" in **Genesis 2:24** means to stick and to stay. Don't allow your in-laws to pull you apart from each other. When you are married you become one flesh in the eyes of God. What God has joined together let no man divide you apart! (**Mark 10:9**) Make sure you leave your family and cleave to your spouse. Don't abandon your family but maintain healthy boundaries. Keep your focus on the one that you committed your vows to. The twelve rules of engagement are important when dealing with our in-laws. Remember that there are no perfect people or perfect families. Make the proper adjustments and use wisdom on how to properly relate to your in-laws.

The Three Toxic In-Law Scenarios

In dealing with our in-laws, there can be three toxic scenario's that may challenge your relationship with your spouse. Beware of these scenarios.

Scenario #1 - Daddy's Little Girl :

In this scenario, the father has a close relationship with his daughter. It is important that the father releases his daughter to develop a healthy relationship with her husband without any interference. Often times, the father is the first male in his daughters life and he views her as his little girl. It is imperative that when the father walks his daughter down the aisle during the wedding ceremony that he is sending the message that he is trusting the groom to be the man in her life. The father must decrease to allow the husband to increase in the life of his daughter. Women, don't allow your father to interfere in your marriage by intimidating your husband. Men, always respect your wife's father and reassure him that you are trustworthy and will take care of his daughter.

Scenario #2 - Momma's Baby Boy:

In this scenario, the mother has a very close knit relationships with her son. The mother may be overly protective and is not willing to give her son's wife the opportunity to develop a close relationship with him. The son of the mother must be very discreet and wise. Do not allow your mother to take the place of your wife. Remember that your wife is first. In most cases, the mother still feels a sense of duty and responsibility to be there for her son. He needs to develop a strong relationship with his wife and not compromise his marriage in order to keep his mother happy. It is important that the wife be patient and not try to compete with her mother-in-law. Establish boundaries in this relationship. You must leave in order to cleave!

Scenario #3 - Sibling Rivalry:

In this scenario, the siblings are in competition with each other. "Anything you can do I can do better!" This mentality of competition was probably developed during childhood. In this case, the husband or wife is constantly trying to prove their worth to siblings. They are living their lives to impress them. This is a very unhealthy relationship and will cause a lot of strain in the marriage. Many arguments and disputes rise up because of the nature of the relationship. This is unacceptable! It is important that both parties deal with all insecurities and jealousy. In the bible Cain killed his brother Abel because of jealousy. Embrace your siblings and celebrate them no matter your situation. Maintain healthy boundaries and stay focused on your own life. Stop competing with each other.

Conclusion

In this fourth battlefield many don't survive. It is tough dealing with in-laws when you are at odds with each other. Strive to develop and maintain a positive relationship with them.

Do not lose your identity trying to fit the expectations of your in-laws. Always respect them but stay true to yourself. All in-laws are not difficult. Try your best to remain positive and discover the best in everyone.

<u>NOTES</u>

CHAPTER 5

BATTLEFIELD #5 - PARENTING

Psalms 127:3-5 *"Lo, children are an heritage of the LORD: and the fruit of the womb is his reward. As arrows are in the hand of a mighty man; so are children of the youth. Happy is the man that hath his quiver full of them: they shall not be ashamed, but they shall speak with the enemies in the gate."*

Parenting is a privilege from the Lord. According to the bible, children are considered a heritage and a reward from God. Many people look forward to having children but do not necessarily count up the cost of parenting. Raising children is not an easy task. It is important that you discuss with your mate their views on raising and parenting children.

There are different styles of parenting. I believe that children are a byproduct of their parents and environment. We often raise our children based on our own upbringing. Do not assume that your mate's experience as a child is the same as yours.

All households are different and parenting styles may differ.

This particular battlefield is a challenge because we do not always agree with how to raise our children. Marriage does not guarantee that you are ready to have children. Some marriages and relationships have blended families and require parenting responsibilities. Sometimes having children can place a strain on the marriage if both parties are not prepared. It is important to pursue parenting with wisdom, knowledge and preparation.

Children can change the dynamic of a relationship. Make sure that parenting is discussed. Get to know how your mate feels about having children. Don't assume that your mate wants to raise children or be a parent. Parenting is serious business and it is not for the faint at heart.

The Four Styles of Parenting

The purpose of this book is to equip you with tools to overcome certain battlefields. If you have children in your current relationship or plan to have children in the future, there are four primary styles of parenting.

80

#1 The Authoritative Style:

This style of parenting is very strict and often controlling. They thrive on obedience and discipline. This particular style basically says, "My way or the highway". There is not much give and take when it comes to expectations and standards with this style. It is all about the rules. You are rewarded for your obedience and disciplined for not doing what you are told.

#2 The Persuasive Style:

The parent tries to communicate with the child about why the rules are in place. They encourage their children to be self-regulated and responsible through constant persuasion. This parenting style sets the standard and then expects the child to follow through by reasoning or be disciplined for disobeying. There is much conversation and follow up to discuss the reasons why things are expected to be done appropriately. Anything that is done out of order is unacceptable and will be followed up.

#3 The Unrestrictive Style:

This style of parenting grants excessive freedom to children. Parents are viewed more like friends than authoritative figures. The kids typically get what they want and the parents are more lenient. Parents try to avoid being viewed as bossy, mean, or critical. The purpose of this style is to avoid confrontation and be less demanding in hopes that the child will do well with less restrictions.

#4 The Independent Style:

This style can be considered neglectful. The parent does not engage the child and allows them to independently make their own decisions. Freedom is their motto! The parent is not motivated to instruct, discipline, or direct the child in the way that they should go. The child is permitted to supervise themselves within the parameters of the parents rules.

These are just a few parental styles that people generally use when raising their children. Which style fits your personality? It is important that you know this about yourself and your spouse. The keyword is "personality". Your personality will determine your parental style. Some parents are confrontational and strict while others are lenient and unrestrictive. Every child is different and certain parental styles may not be effective for them. Be willing to try different styles.

The Five D's of Parenting

It is important that you have a system and style when parenting. Children are a byproduct of their parents. We must take full responsibility for how they are raised and strive to help them in their development. There are Five D's of Parenting that can assist in your child's development.

#1 Devotion:

I Corinthians 13:13 NIV *"And now these three remain: faith, hope and love. But the greatest of these is love."*

It is said that love covers a multitude of faults. Our homes should be filled with love and devotion. Our children must know that we love them. Take the time to show them affection. Spend time with your children and remember to hug, kiss and reassure them.

#2 Direction:

Proverbs 22:6 *"Train up a child in the way he should go: and when he is old, he will not depart from it."*

Psalms 127:4 *"As arrows are in the hand of a mighty man; so are children of the youth."*

Our kids are our responsibility. It is important that we direct them. Every good parent must be willing to train their children by leading them in the right direction. Remember that you are raising an adult and not maintaining a child. One day your child will become an adult. Our children are like arrows in our hands. We must use our parenting as a bow to aim, stretch, pull, and launch them into the right direction to succeed.

#3 Discipline:

Proverbs 29:15 *"The rod and reproof give wisdom: but a child left to himself bringeth his mother to shame."*

Children should never be left to raise themselves. We must be willing to guide them. Any child that grows up without any discipline will have a difficult time succeeding in life. Never confuse discipline with abuse. Abusing our children can lead to residual effects that can negatively impact their adult life. Healthy discipline should encourage balance, love, character and good decisions.

#4 Demonstration:

I Corinthians 11:1 "*Be ye followers of me, even as I also am of Christ.*"

Living by the saying, "Do what I say and not as I do", is not wise. Our children need us to demonstrate what we expect them to do on a daily basis. Be real with your children. Don't set standards and expectations that you are not willing to live or demonstrate in front of them. Demonstration is the best teacher that you can give to your child. Remember that they hear what we say but see what we do!

#5 Determination:

2 Timothy 4:7 "*I have fought a good fight, I have finished my course, I have kept the faith.*"

Keep the faith and never give up on your children. They may not always do what you ask them to do but keep on loving them. There are no perfect parents or children. It is okay to acknowledge this fact to each other. Parenting is not an easy task or responsibility. Remember that you are not raising a robot. You are parenting a human being! Be determined to not give up. Stand with your child through thick and thin.

Determination will encourage you to finish strong and be there for them no matter what.

Dealing with a Blended Family

One of the challenges of a blended family is raising children from a previous relationship. If not handled properly, a blended family can present many challenges.

Marrying someone with children is a package deal. If the children are young, there is an expectation that you may have to play an active parental role in their lives even though you are not the biological parent.

Maintain a standard when it comes to your children. It is important that you set boundaries and expectations for your family. There are a number of questions that need to be asked in order to determine the parenting responsibilities and roles within a blended family.

#1 "Is the biological parent still involved?"

#2 "Is there social and financial support for the child?"

#3 "Has closure been established with the Ex?"

#4 "Who has custody of the child?"

#5 "What is my role in the child's life?"

#6 "Does the child call me mommy/daddy or something else?"

#7 "Is the Ex aware of my role in the child's life?"

#8 "What is our plan to successfully raise our children as one family unit?"

These are just a few questions that you should ask to generate a discussion concerning a blended family. Remember to use wisdom and be honest and open about how you feel. If you are not the biological parent of the child please do not force yourself on them. This is not wise. Take your time and develop a relationship with the child. Never compare yourself or disrespect the biological parent of the child. This will not make you look good in the long run. Be yourself and don't try to be someone else.

Being a stepparent can be awkward. Do everything in your power to treat the child in a loving manner. Try your best to avoid indifference with all the children. Communicate with your spouse about how you feel about your roles as parents. Remember that a blended family doesn't have to be a divided house. Love covers all!

Avoid The Baby Mama & Daddy Drama

Try your best to stay clear of drama from the previous relationship of your spouse or significant other! One of the biggest mistakes that couples make is disputing and fighting people from past relationships. Set a standard and allow the child to have a relationship with their biological parents without any drama. Focus your energy on your child and not the negativity. Remember that you are no longer in a romantic relationship with the biological parent of the child. Engage your Ex in a healthy manner and avoid negative situations with them.

Conclusion

This battlefield can only be overcome through communication, love, patience and understanding. Parenting is an honor and privilege. There are many people that cannot have children. Do not take it for granted. Remember that your children are your assignment and you must complete your mission by loving them!

NOTES

CHAPTER 6

BATTLEFIELD #6 - DOMESTIC SUPPORT

Mark 3:25 *"And if a house be divided against itself, that house cannot stand."*

Making Your House a Home

Domestic support is very important when it comes to marriage. The primary focus should be to build a home with standards and morals. Your home should be a safe place for the entire family. It is important to establish a culture that is filled with peace, love and security.

The home should not be a toxic place. Take the time and effort to create an environment where everyone feels supported. The safest place on the planet should be your home. Making a house a home is a deliberate effort. Everyone in the household should be involved in the process.

Five Areas of Domestic Support

There are five Domestic Support Areas needed to build a strong home. It will take the efforts of everyone to produce success in the home. Meet and communicate with your family the need to work together as a team to establish strong domestic support for each other.

Domestic Support Area #1 - Vision

Proverbs 29:18 *"Where there is no vision, the people perish: but he that keepeth the law, happy is he."*

Proverbs 29:18 shares the importance of having a vision. A vision for the home will lead to a productive path. What are our dreams? Where do we see ourselves within the next 5 to 10 years? What are our goals and objectives to obtain our vision? How long will it take for us to get there? These are just a few of the questions that every family needs to ask when it comes to vision and planning for the future.

It is imperative that the entire family understands there is a vision for the house. As a couple, take the time to plan your goals together. Remember that a dream can get you started but discipline will keep you going! Planning your dreams and goals are paramount when it comes to fulfilling your vision. The Bible says in *Habakkuk 2:2,3* *"And the LORD answered me, and said, Write the vision, and make it plain upon tables, that he may run that readeth it. For the vision is yet for an appointed time, but at the end it shall speak, and not lie: though it tarry, wait for it; because it will surely come, it will not tarry."* Make sure you write, read and run with your plan and vision. Whenever we fail to plan, we plan to fail. *Jeremiah 29:11 NIV"For I know the plans I have for you," declares the LORD, "plans to prosper you and not to harm you, plans to give you hope and a future."* Take the time to make a plan and set your goals. A vision will allow you to see whether or not your family is going in the right direction.

Domestic Support Area #2 - Economics

Finances are always a priority when it comes to domestic support. We often hear the saying, "There can be no romance without finance." This may not always be true but money certainly is important in a relationship. Economics is the foundation that gives a sense of security and stability.

Here are a few things to consider when it comes to economics in the home:

#1) Adequate Steady Financial Income

Cash flow is important when it comes to domestic support. Find ways to establish multiple streams of income to avoid being broke.

#2) Budget and Save for the Future

Make sure you tell your money where you want it to go. Don't overspend and waste any finances. Save for your future and legacy. Establish an emergency fund for tough times. Remember to save for retirement.

#3) Maintain Bills & Utilities

It is important that all bills are maintained for the safety and security of your family. Your family needs gas, electricity, and water. Avoid collections and shut-offs. Guard your FICO Score and financial future by maintaining good credit.

#4) Maintain Health Coverage

Always make sure that your family can get the medical assistance that they need. It can be a matter of life or death. Never risk the health of your family.

#5) Life Insurance and a Will

Provided a death benefit for the ones that you love. It is a gift that you can give when you leave the planet. Do your best to not leave bills and financial burdens for your family when you are gone. Purchase a Life Insurance Policy and establish a Will to carry out your final wishes.

#6) Real Estate and Investments

A wealthy man once told me, "Everyone should own a piece of the earth!" There can be no true wealth without land or some form of Real Estate. Purchase some real estate that you can call yours. Don't be afraid to invest for the future of your family.

Domestic Support Area #3 - Environment

The physical surroundings of your home will often determine your success. Focus on keeping the house clean. Maintaining the yard and repairs throughout the property is important. Be organized and diligent to the best of your ability. All of these things contribute to domestic support. The physical environment of a home has nothing to do with any gender specific responsibilities. It is important that the entire family work together to maintain a good physical environment.

Domestic Support Area #4 - Provision

We cannot fulfill our vision without provision. This area focuses on shopping for the necessities like food, clothing and medicine. Your family has needs. Never confuse your wants with your needs. Sit down and discuss what your needs are for the home and family. An example is being determined to keep water, electricity, groceries, supplies and food etc. in your home at all times.

Domestic Support Area #5 - Atmosphere

The atmosphere of a home is not just about the physical surroundings but it is about the way it makes you feel! Is there peace in your home? Are you able to rest and relax? What about love and happiness? All of these things will not be obtained by purchasing furniture, carpet and clothes. The ambience of your home sets the atmosphere and impacts the soul of everyone who enters that environment. Maintain your atmosphere!

Conclusion

Domestic support is a two way street. In order to overcome this battlefield, neither party can be selfish or self-centered. Be determined to focus on the needs of each other. Remember that charity begins at home and then spreads abroad. Do not neglect your home!

<u>NOTES</u>

CHAPTER 7

BATTLEFIELD #7 - TIME

Ecclesiastes 3:1 *"To every thing there is a season, and a time to every purpose under the heaven."*

Everything has a time and a season. All of us must recognize that time is a gift from GOD. It equates to life and we should make the best of it. It is imperative that we understand that marriage and relationships take time to develop. There is absolutely no time to waste. Prioritize your time by developing your marriage and relationship.

Quality versus Quantity

Marriage needs proper time investment to succeed. Never confuse quality with quantity. Quantity deals with how much time you spend while quality focuses on how that time is spent. If you are not able to give a lot of time make sure it is quality time.

Do not underestimate the power of quality time. Remember to plan your outings. It does not have to be difficult or complex. Plan with simplicity and be creative and thoughtful. Make every effort to pay attention to details and plan your best.

Many couples make the mistake of confusing quantity with quality. Spending much time with each other is important but maximizing the moment produces a greater impact in the relationship. How to maximize the moment? Make sure that the time you spend with each other is memorable and impactful. Do not fall into the "slump of do nothing". The lack of spending quality time with each other can lead to feeling distant and unappreciated. Combat the slump by communicating and spending quality time with each other.

Me & We Time

In every relationship there should be "Me & We" time. Spending time alone and focusing on yourself is called "Me Time". Loving your spouse but not taking care of yourself is irresponsible. It is impossible to love on others effectively if you do not take care of yourself. Take the time to engage in activities that promote self-worth and well-being. Go to the salon, barbershop, spa, gym or park. Do whatever it takes to feel good. Remember to make time for yourself.

Making time for your spouse by planning a date night, vacation or stay-cation is called "We Time". This is an opportunity where you can pour into your spouse. Block off some space in your calendar and agenda and do something together. This is not about the children or any outside influences. It is okay to have close friends around as long as the both of you are in agreement and your friends do not take the attention away from your spouse. Make it your priority to enjoy each other.

Family Time

Family time is important. Be deliberate in scheduling time with your children and family. Try to schedule a family day at least once a week. This will give your family the opportunity to spend quality time with each other. Scheduling an outing like a movie and dinner, or stay home and play board games are all great activities. Establish a budget for a family vacation. This will give you some great memories and will build unity and closeness among yourselves.

The Eight Time Stages of a Marriage

There are several stages within a marriage cycle. Understanding these stages will help you to overcome the battlefield of time. It is imperative that you identify your marriage stage in order to succeed and grow. Do not compare yourself to other marriages because all marriages are not in the same stage or season. Timing is everything!

Time Stage #1 - The Courtship Stage

This is the honeymoon stage of the relationship. Love is in the air and no one can do anything wrong. There is a lot of dating and spending quality time with each other. This stage caters to one another's feelings and fantasy. The attraction is there as well as the desire to connect whenever possible. There is a strong desire to be around each other all of the time. Your partner is considered to be the priority above everything else.

Time Stage #2 - The Commitment Stage

Both parties are determined to be committed to each other. This stage reveals the intentions of the relationship. Many couples decide to be exclusive or get engaged and prepare for marriage. They decide to exclusively date their love interest. Some couples make the decision to get married and build a life with the one they love.

Time Stage #3 - The Critical Stage

The couple gets married and lives together. They discover their differences and dislikes. The honeymoon stage is over! They become more critical and arguments become more persistent after moving in with each other. Some people give up at this stage while others allow their love and commitment to get them through. The Critical Stage is temporary. This is an opportunity for the couple to get to know each other in a more intimate and personal way. They are learning the pros and cons of living with their spouse. This is the stage of discovery of two people becoming one.

Time Stage #4 - The Compromise Stage

In order to succeed in marriage there must be some compromise. You must be willing to give up something in order to support your spouse. Compromise is not always comfortable. Sometimes you will feel like you are receiving the short end of the stick. Please understand that you must sacrifice some things for the greater good of your marriage. Two people becoming one without any compromise is impossible! Anyone that does not want to compromise in a relationship should remain single. This stage is about being unselfish and sacrificing for the benefit of the marriage.

Time Stage #5 - The Creative Stage

This stage is filled with new things. Perhaps, you are expecting a new baby, launching a career or business, or even relocating and moving into a new home. All of these scenarios are in the Creative Stage. Sometimes couples may feel like two passing ships. There's not a lot of time spent with each other because of the busyness of the day. This stage may produce more money and success but lead to distance and strain in a relationship. The lack of time invested in relationship development could stifle the couple's connection with each other. Don't allow the creation of new things to drive you apart and avoid competing with each other.

Time Stage #6 - The Cooperation Stage

Cooperation is not like compromise which implies that someone is giving up something. The Cooperation Stage suggests a balance of give and take. It is about a "win-win" situation. This stage is for mature couples. There are less arguments and debates. There is more unity. They know each other well and what buttons not to push. They live with the philosophy, "we do it better together"!

Time Stage #7 - The Completion Stage

This is a season that is full of accomplishments. The children become adults, the mortgage has been paid off, and they are financially stable. This is a stage when a couple can look back and appreciate what they've accomplished together over the years. This stage may present "empty nest syndrome". This is when your life was dedicated to taking care of the children and maintaining a family that is no longer in the home. It is important that married couples build a healthy relationship with each other in the absence of their children. One day your children will leave and establish their own family. What will you have left when they leave? Do you still feel significant? Is your spouse still valuable to you? Even though you have completed many things in this stage, do you still complete each other? This can be a time of rediscovery and recommitment. There is nothing wrong with restarting the Courtship Stage at this point.

Time Stage #8 - The Cruising Stage

This stage exemplifies longevity in a marriage. Take this time to cruise through life with the one you love. This is not the stage where you are overworking yourselves and trying establishing new things. This is a wonderful opportunity to do whatever you want to do with the one you love. Make it your priority to grow old together in this stage. Enjoy this time by gracefully moving at your own pace. Hopefully you have saved money and have taken the time to prepare. The cruising stage is all about you and your spouse taking 100% of your time to maximize every moment in life and enjoying it to the fullest together.

Conclusion

The battlefield of time is all about establishing priorities. Once your priorities are set then start the planning phase. Take the time to establish balance in every area of your life. Do not neglect your spouse or family. Remember that Life is too short and time is always moving!

NOTES

_____

_____

_____

_____

_____

_____

_____

_____

_____

_____

_____

_____

_____

_____

_____

CHAPTER 8

WE FIGHT BETTER TOGETHER!

Ephesians 6:12 NIV *"For our struggle is not against flesh and blood, but against the rulers, against the authorities, against the powers of this dark world and against the spiritual forces of evil in the heavenly realms."*

All Marriages have Challenges.

Never feel like you are the only marriage experiencing problems. It is not easy to become one with an individual. Many couples use their energy to fight each other instead of partnering to find solutions to their problems. Always have one another's back no matter what you may face. There will be tough times but standing together will determine how victorious your marriage will be during the trials of life.

A wedding does not guarantee happiness or marital bliss. After every wedding there is a marriage. Many couples plan elegant and grand weddings but fail to plan their marriage and life together. Good marriages are made! Couples must be deliberate in building a successful marriage. There are spiritual and natural forces that will try to hinder your marriage. Always fight for your marriage no matter what happens.

Over 50 percent of marriages end in divorce. This statistic is an indicator that many couples are taking the option of separation and divorce rather than sticking and staying with each other. Don't be afraid to fight in the areas of attack that the enemy seemingly is getting the best of you. Fight for your family! Stop lying to yourself about the condition of your relationship. Give yourself permission to make real change.

It is important that you fight for your marriage together. This is not an easy task. Both parties must be willing to cooperate with each other. There are five things that couples most do to support each other.

#1 Be Honest.

James 5:16 *"Confess your faults one to another, and pray one for another, that ye may be healed. The effectual fervent prayer of a righteous man availeth much."*

Honesty in a marriage is very pivotal. It is important that you do not lie to yourself or to each other. Identify all of the issues and problems that are hindering your marriage. Many couples continue to live a lie and never confess their faults to each other. Living a lie is a disservice to your relationship. It is impossible to make any changes without honesty in the relationship. It is imperative that the brokenness of the relationship is acknowledged. We cannot fix what we are not willing to acknowledge. Being honest in your relationship will allow you the freedom to make change.

Your spouse deserves the truth. Do not live a double life. Pretending that you are happy with your relationship will only make things worse. Be honest and tell the truth. Get rid of the skeletons in the closet. There is healing in honesty even though the truth may hurt. Allow your relationship with your spouse to be liberated and not be in bondage due to lies and dishonesty.

#2 Be Forgiving.

Matthew 6:15 *"But if ye forgive not men their trespasses, neither will your Father forgive your trespasses."*

Forgiving your spouse can be very challenging. Many relationships have ended due to unforgiveness. Every relationship is different. Please understand that forgiveness is a gift to yourself. Unforgiveness will always betray you. It is not your friend. Sometimes we refused to forgive others because we want them to feel our pain. Unforgiveness will not only hurt them but it will hurt you as well. Choosing not to forgive someone is like cutting yourself with a knife and wanting the other person to bleed.

Accepting the apology of your spouse and allowing them the opportunity to change will help you both to have a stronger bond. Be careful how you treat one another in order to not hinder your prayers. **1 Peter 3:7** *"Likewise, ye husbands, dwell with them according to knowledge, giving honour unto the wife, as unto the weaker vessel, and as being heirs together of the grace of life; that your prayers be not hindered."* How you treat one another is very important. Forgiveness is the foundation for change, healing and reconciliation. Be willing to forgive your spouse even if others refuse. Remember that you have a right to forgive without the approval of others.

#3 Get Wise Counsel.

Proverbs 11:14 *"Where no counsel is, the people fall: but in the multitude of counsellors there is safety."*

Surround yourself with wise counsel. It is imperative that you seek after great advice. Take the time to improve on your relationship by reading, attending conferences, and getting counseling. Find successful couples and connect with them. There is no need to try to reinvent the wheel. Obtain the best advice and apply it in your relationship. Don't be afraid to invest in getting professional counseling. Allow yourself to be accountable to wise counselors.

#4 Do the Work!

Matthew 5:16 *"Let your light so shine before men, that they may see your good works, and glorify your Father which is in heaven."*

Fighting for your marriage requires hard work. Do not expect anything to come easily. There are principles that must be put into action. Stop talking about doing better and just do it! It may take some time adjusting to change. Working on yourself and your relationship is worth the time that is invested.

Try your best to be productive everyday. Do whatever you have to do in order to improve your marriage. This may require time and sweat equity! Be consistent and deliberate in putting in the work. Doing the heavy lifting will reveal the necessary progress overtime. There is no easy road or shortcuts when it comes to fighting for your marriage. Remember if you do the work, you will reap the benefits!

#5 Don't Stop Fighting!

1 Timothy 6:12 *"Fight the good fight of faith, lay hold on eternal life, whereunto thou art also called, and hast professed a good profession before many witnesses."*

No matter what happens..."Don't stop fighting"! The foundation of your fight should be the love that you have for each other. Love is not weak but it is very strong. Sometimes you may have to fight by yourself. Never assume that both parties are willing to fight for the marriage. One may be motivated and the other me feel like throwing in the towel and calling it quits! Do not give up on your spouse. Being willing to go all the way. Learn strategies that will give you leverage in every situation. Communication is the key. Always remember to keep your communication lines open. Verbalize your desire to keep the marriage together. Pray and ask GOD for wisdom. Your marriage is worth fighting for.

Conclusion

Always remember that you are a team. Be willing to fulfill your vows that you made to each other. All the battlefields that you may face in marriage is not easy to overcome. Make sure that you do not fight against each other. You are on the same team and should be striving for the same goals. A win for one is a win for all. A successful marriage should be a benefit for both of you. Fight the good fight of faith and overcome your challenges together because you fight better together!

NOTES

A FINAL WORD

There are battlefields that we all must face and overcome in marriage. Apply the principles in this book to make your marriage amazing!

After every wedding there is a marriage. Our marriages exemplify the sum total of our actions. If you are single and are looking for love, please use the wisdom in this book. Be willing to fight for your relationship and never give up. There will be challenges as well as mistakes. Do not give up! Be determined and keep it moving. YOU WILL OVERCOME!

Made in the USA
Columbia, SC
14 September 2020